LIST BUILDING STRATEGIES FOR AFFILIATE MARKETERS

ANTHONY EKANEM

Contents

Preface

List building is all about connecting with your target audience by offering them high-quality information in exchange for their subscription, and in affiliate marketing, a targeted and responsive email list will be the critical element to your success.

Once a subscriber is a confirmed member of your list, you can begin sending promotional based follow-up emails in balance with relevant and useful content based on your overall market.

Email marketers collect leads using a combination of squeeze pages and opt-in forms. These forms are generated by your autoresponder provider and are embedded into the HTML code of your squeeze page template.

Each time a visitor to your squeeze page enters in their name and email address, they are added to your mailing list database and become an active subscriber of your newsletter.

List building helps facilitate the process of converting subscribers into active customers since once your prospect has been added to your mailing list, you can develop a relationship with them. This will encourage sales as well as repeat sales (which will make up the larger majority of your email marketing income).

CHAPTER ONE

The Tools You Need

To begin building a profitable email marketing campaign; however, you will need to make sure that you have all of the tools that are required, including:

1) Professional Autoresponder Account

With autoresponder services like www.Aweber.com and www.GetResponse.com, you can set up an unlimited number of mailing lists, each one featuring customised code that serves as your opt-in box.

By segmenting your lists, you will be able to tailor your emails so that they directly communicate with targeted groups of subscribers who are interested in specific information or topics.

An autoresponder is a mailing list system set up with pre-loaded messages due to go out at scheduled times. This means that you can write all of your messages at once but have them trickle out to your subscribers on various days. ·

Being able to pre-create this content makes life a lot easier as an email marketer. This is because you can set it up on auto-pilot and spend your time and effort driving traffic to your squeeze page to expand your list continuously.

The autoresponder service provider you choose will provide you with an account where you can log in and create unlimited email campaigns as well. This means that you can cater to a dozen or more niche markets but keep things organised and well managed by emailing these groups individually to avoid confusion.

For instance, perhaps you are interested in the dog training niche market as well as the golfing market. You would create two autoresponder campaigns. One titled *golfing* and one titled *dog training*.

You would create your content separately for these two markets, pre-fill your autoresponder account, and it would instantly send out your notices, news and updates to each group of subscribers.

2) Squeeze Page

A squeeze page houses your opt-in form and provides a place for your contacts to find you, evaluate what you are offering and decide to become an active subscriber of your list.

A squeeze page is very similar to a sales page in terms of its primary function, which is to pull in customers and motivate them to take action, in this case, subscribe to your list. That call to action is <u>essential</u>in creating high-performance squeeze pages, and you must place emphasis on ensuring that your visitors are directed to fill in the opt-in form; otherwise they will not be added to your list.

You need to direct visitors to enter their name and email address as well as instruct them to confirm their request to join your list (if you are using double opt-in).

One thing to keep in mind when developing your squeeze page is that it should motivate visitors in the same way that a traditional sales page should; however, the actual structure of your squeeze page will be very different.

With sales pages, they are typically designed to offer as much information about a particular product or service as possible, since the main focus is on transforming a visitor into a customer.

With a squeeze page, you aren't asking your visitor to decide to purchase or commit to anything other than to subscribe to your mailing list where they are rewarded with a free product.

Keeping this offer or giveaway in mind, when you develop a squeeze page, you need to have a strong focus on your market, and design your offer around an existing problem, need or question.

To come up with the best incentive offer possible, you'll need to thoroughly evaluate your market, as well as competing offers so that you can create a relevant product that is in demand and likely to capture attention from your target audience.

Squeeze pages should be designed to offer a clear navigation system, basic structure and template and a compelling offer.

To summarise, your list building funnel consists of three major parts:

1: Squeeze Page With Opt-In Form
2: Compelling High-Quality Offer or Incentive
3: Follow Up Emails And Broadcasts

We will discuss the anatomy of a successful squeeze page in an upcoming chapter so that you can begin to develop your own.

3) Giveaway (Incentive)

Your giveaway is the most essential element on your squeeze page.

If your offer doesn't motivate visitors into subscribing, all of your marketing efforts will be lost. This means that you need your offer to be of interest to the majority of your target market, rather than to a small group of subscribers. The higher the quality of your giveaway, as well as the more relevant your offer, is to your market, the easier it will be to recruit new subscribers.

There are many different ways to ensure that the product you are giving away is of a high-perceived value by your subscriber base and is likely to be successful in converting new subscribers.

To start, consider the different types of products that are being successfully sold in online marketplaces and create a shorter version of a hot selling product, and offer it for free to anyone who subscribes to your list.

If competitors are successful in selling a similar product and you are giving away a high-quality product based on the same topic, imagine just how easy it will be to recruit visitors and subscribers to your site.

And better yet, what better way to begin building a relationship with an active subscriber base than by offering them something of equal value with no strings (or price tag) attached!

You could offer:

- Free Reports
- Free Ebooks (full length of leaked chapters)
- Free Tutorial Guides
- Video Tutorials
- Free or Trial Access To a Membership Program
- Free Booklet with "Top Tips"
- Free Weekly Newsletter Subscription
- Free templates or graphics
- Free Audio Interviews, Lessons, Tutorials

The key to creating a successful giveaway product is its overall relevance and existing demand.

You want to make sure that your target audience is actively searching for similar information, and that it is being sold successfully in the marketplace. If you do that, you will have little difficulty building a massive list of targeted prospects who will be eager to receive your emails and broadcasts.

If you plan to promote an ebook or e-course of some kind, a robust method of building a massive mailing list while generating new business for your product is by offering a leaked chapter of your information product.

By offering this free chapter, you can provide new subscribers with a sample of the quality of your work, as well as generate buzz around your upcoming product launch.

If your product is well written, you will find it exceptionally easy to build a subscriber base of people who will likely purchase the full-length version when it launches.

This is also a savvy method of creating a viral campaign for your upcoming launch as people pass around the 'leaked chapter' to everyone they know.

If you are interested in outsourcing your project to experienced freelancers, you can easily find a trustworthy professional from the following freelance marketplaces:

http://www.Guru.com

http://www.Elance.com

http://www.Scriptlance.com

4) Domain And Hosting Accounts

There are many different domain registrars available to choose from. One thing to keep in mind; however, is that you should have a good idea as to the niche or market that you are intending on targeting before registering your domain. That way, you can register a domain name that incorporates relevant keywords about that target audience.

For instance, if you want to build a mailing list that targets the work-at-home job niche, consider registering a domain name that incorporates the keywords *'legit online jobs'*, where you would offer a free report on how to find legitimate work-at-home jobs. The domain and the content both speak directly to your target audience.

To streamline your ability to build targeted lists, you also need a web hosting account, making it easy to capture your visitor's information and add them to your list by showcasing a squeeze or landing page.

When it comes to choosing a hosting provider, you need to make sure that you go with a service that allows for flexibility and fast upgrades. You can start with a smaller package, and as your marketing expands, you can upgrade your account to a larger package.

With your hosting provider, make sure that they offer the ability to use sub-domains so that you can create multiple interior pages for every squeeze page you create.

CHAPTER TWO

Creating A High Converting Squeeze Page

This is where it all begins; creating a high converting squeeze page that directly communicates with your target audience and motivates them into subscribing to your list. By providing reliable information and relevant content, you will quickly begin to establish credibility with your list members and a reputation as someone interested in providing high-quality information and exceptional value.

A squeeze page is NOT designed to sell. Its primary job is to convert traffic into confirmed subscribers, and you need to keep this in mind when creating your page. All you need is a simple HTML page you can set up on your website or blog on sites such as http://www.Wordpress.comor http://www.Blogger.com.

There are even free plugins for websites that are designed on the WordPress platform that will automatically insert an opt-in form on your website. One of these services is available at http://www.CodeBanter.com. To help you create the most effective squeeze page possible, here is a quick overview of the essential elements that you need to include in your squeeze page:

1. Compelling, Attention-Grabbing Headlines

Your squeeze page's headline should be the very first thing that your visitor sees and therefore it needs to attract attention, draw them in and keep them focused long enough for them to become a confirmed subscriber of your mailing list.

Your headlines text size should be larger than the rest of the text on your page, and for increased exposure, consider adding colour to your headline (red and blue works well). You could also consider highlighting your headline and any sub-headline that you use. You can use the <h1> and <h2> tags to enlarge your text, which will not only help with capturing attention from your visitors but will also alert search engine crawlers that the expanded text is essential.

Centre your headline within your template and work in your opt-in box so that it is close to the headline. If you are using a CSS based squeeze page, your opt-in box could be placed in the right column, with a bullet list of benefits featured in the main body of your page.

2. Content/Body

You should keep your content trimmed down so that it focuses only on the essential information that you have to share. Avoid wordy squeeze pages that offer endless paragraphs of information. Your squeeze page has ONLY one task, to convert visitors into subscribers and so you need to keep it clear, concise and of course, exciting!

You will want to split test your copy (including lengths) to determine what will increase conversion rates. But in the meantime, here is a quick overview of how to structure your squeeze page content better so that it is easy to read, understand and encourages subscriptions:

1) Use Bullet Points To Highlight Benefits

Bullet points emphasise important features and draw attention to the distinctive aspects of becoming a subscriber to your list. This is a great way to showcase the benefits of becoming a subscriber, and what they will receive, in return, for their subscription.

For example, if you were offering a report on the *'Insider Secrets to Finding a Work At Home Job'*, your benefits list could include:

- Find out how to land a high paying telecommuting job even if you have absolutely no experience online!

- Avoid devastating work at home job scams that circulate the industry and target people just like you!

- Discover the #1 freelance website where 99.9% of new telecommuters can secure employment in their first week online.

- Create a compelling resume that guarantees you stand out from the crowd and get noticed by top-paying companies online!

2) Retain Focus At ALL Times

Eliminate any external links and keep your squeeze page focused. You want to avoid distractions in directing potential subscribers to external websites (or even internal pages on your site). Their ONLY option should be to subscribe to your mailing list. You don't want to confuse them or deter them from your one objective; getting that lead.

Avoid navigation menus, widgets, plugins, or links to articles. Your squeeze page should be one page long, feature your bullet list, headline, opt-in box and private policy. Eliminate clutter and any information or content that is not necessary to secure the subscriber.

3) Strong & Clear Call To Action

If you want your squeeze page to recruit new subscribers successfully, you NEED to direct visitors to fill out your opt-in form and confirm their request. Do NOT assume that people know what to do. Remember, not everyone is likely to have experience with mailing lists, and so you need to directly instruct them as to how they can gain access to your free, high-quality offer. Just the same way, you also want to direct them to confirm their request to your list once they have entered in their name and email address.

If you are using a double opt-in format, you will NOT be able to communicate with subscribers who have not verified their request, so make sure that you are following up and instructing everyone to confirm. You can do this by automatically directing subscribers to a secondary page on your site. That page thanks them for subscribing and tells them that the final step is to check their email and confirm their request to join your list by clicking on the verification link sent out by your autoresponder system.

Just like your squeeze page, keep your confirmation page clean and crisp. Avoid ANY external links at this point because you need your subscriber to follow your instructions instantly, eliminating any chance of their forgetting to confirm.

Your Incentive Offer

To entice your website visitors into subscribing to your autoresponder, you want to take the time to consider a **free incentive** to maximise the number of visitors that you can convert into subscribers.

People are often cautious about handing over their name and email address to a stranger. With so many Email Marketers spamming their lists with useless garbage, web users have become careful about whose lists they join. **This is why you need to present an irresistible offer.**

You want to stand out from the crowd by taking them by the hand and saying *"Look at what I can offer you!"*, and in case they aren't listening, a free incentive may be the push they need to motivate them to take action and subscribe to your list. It's a compelling way to generate a massive list of valid opt-in readers as well as begin the process of building a relationship with these subscribers.

When it comes to what you should offer your visitors, there are many different products format that works well, depending on your niche market.

You could offer:

- Free Report
- Free eBooks
- Free Graphic Packages
- Free Tutorials
- Free Sample Chapter (from a paid product)

- Free e-Courses

You want to spend some time evaluating your options when it comes to the giveaway (otherwise called a 'bribe') because it ultimately will be responsible for whether your squeeze page converts or fails. When deciding on a squeeze page incentive, you want to determine what your target market is actually looking for, and only giving them a high-quality product that they can't find anywhere else. You can do this with a free report, eBook or a simple e-course that is set up to deliver training tools and resources weekly.

CHAPTER THREE

Promoting Your Squeeze Page For Maximum Profits

Once you have your squeeze page set up and your autoresponder account created, you need to focus on developing an email sequence that is activated from the moment a website visitor becomes a subscriber.

This is how it works:

Your visitor enters in their information via your squeeze page and confirms their request to be added to your newsletter. Your autoresponder kicks in and emails your prospect a welcome email that you have written. This is sent out automatically within minutes of their subscription.

Your autoresponder continues to email your subscribers on pre-set dates, according to the system you set up within your autoresponder account. You can determine delivery dates and times from your administration panel, and all of the emails you create within your autoresponder account will be sent out to all active subscribers on a regular schedule.

Example: You create four emails that are scheduled to be delivered accordingly:

- **1st Email:**instantly sent to your subscriber thanking them for subscribing to your list and provides the download that you initially offered on your squeeze page, usually a direct link to the download location on your website.
- **2nd Email:**Scheduled to be sent out on the third day after your subscriber has confirmed their request, and includes an email offering free content, additional articles or another report.
- **3rd Email:**Scheduled to go out on the 7th day of the sequence, promotional based, advertising a related product.
- **4th Email:**Scheduled to go out on the 10th day.. and so on.

The balance that you use, when mixing up free content with promotional based material is entirely up to you. However, the more value you give to your list, the easier and faster it will be to develop a relationship with your subscribers.

Taking an aggressive approach to email marketing works for some, however, for the majority, it's always best to tread carefully, initially focusing on building a relationship with your list, and then doubling that up with promotional offers, or recommendations to affiliate based products.

You want to 'condition' your list so that they grow accustomed to receiving promotional based emails from you regularly. It's up to you to keep a pulse on your subscriber base and determine what works best, how frequently you contact them, and whether they respond well to the products you are promoting. Just don't be afraid to experiment and test out new ideas and innovative ways to grow and maintain your subscriber base consistently.

Here are a few ways to build the highest performing mailing lists, quickly and easily:

Create Multiple Squeeze Pages

Rather than just constructing one squeeze page, consider creating a network of opt-in pages that cover various markets as well as the SAME market, but offering a different giveaway product. By doing this, you can cater to all sorts of people who might not be interested in one giveaway but would gladly sign up to receive another. Plus, you can easily split test different layouts and templates by running various squeeze page offers at once. Keep in mind that the more squeeze pages you have in circulation, the more exposure you'll receive.

Note: You can use the same autoresponder sequences for all of your squeeze pages within the same niche markets, as long as you customise the introductory email so that it features each unique giveaway/offer.

Implement Your Squeeze Page Into Social Profiles

If you have a Squidoo lens, you can now add opt-in pages right into your existing page. It's available as a module, and it's a great way to generate instant traffic to a remotely hosted opt-in page. You can set up an unlimited number of Squidoo lens pages, incorporating your squeeze page into each one. Just make sure to make sufficient content into your lens so that you are offering something of value to visitors.

Note: Squidoo is considered an authority website and carries exceptional weight within the search engines. Not only will you be able to generate fresh leads from your opt-in page, but you could also add links to your Squidoo lens pages that lead visitors to your other squeeze pages as well.

Hub Pages is also another great method of drawing in new traffic and subscribers. HubPages works similarly to Squidoo in terms of being able to create single instant websites even if you are unfamiliar with HTML.

http://www.Squidoo.com
   http://www.HubPages.com

You should also add your squeeze page into your www.twitter.comprofile, as well as every other social community you are a part of including Facebook, YouTube and MySpace.

Article Marketing

Article marketing is a very effective (and free!) marketing strategy, and for many of us end up being our primary force behind generating consistent traffic to our squeeze pages. Article marketing is all about offering high quality, relevant content that targets your market and propels them into investigating your resource box and visiting your website to find out more about you.

Article marketing is straightforward to set up, and even if you aren't a proficient writer, you can easily outsource article creation to affordable, high-quality writers. Even if your budget is small, there is no reason why you can't compile a small package of articles, spanning from 300-500 words in length that are highly targeted and relevant to your squeeze page's topic.

Start by submitting 3-5 articles every week, and before you know it, your article campaign will generate consistent traffic to your squeeze pages. As you continue to expand on the number of articles in circulation, you will be able to generate more traffic regularly. Just make sure that the articles you do submit into article directories are exceptionally well written and targeted. After all, these articles represent you and your brand, and you want your readers to be impressed with the quality as they are likely going to base your other products on the information found within your article content.

Pay attention when constructing your author's resource box (which is attached to each article that you submit.)
This resource box is the only place in which you are allowed to include external links, and you want to add a call to action that motivates your reader into clicking on your link and visiting your squeeze page. You also want to use anchor text whenever possible, so that not only are you able to generate traffic from article directories, but you can also rank for specific keywords within the search engines.

Here are a few article directories to get started:

http://www.EzineArticles.com
   http://www.GoArticles.com
   http://www.ArticleDashboard.com

Conclusion

Split testing squeeze pages is an essential element of a successful email marketing campaign. Regardless of how well you design your website, or how thoroughly you analyse each section of your squeeze page, there is no way that you will be able to accurately predict how well your visitors will respond to your offer, without **comparatively testing alternative layouts.**

One easy method of testing your pages and evaluating conversion rates is by using Google's Website Optimiser, a free tool that will help you run simple split tests of any websites you own. You can sign up for a free account at http://www.google.com/analytics/

Develop Your Brand!

It's important to build brand awareness and develop a relationship with your subscriber base, because the more that your list members trust you and the product recommendations that you make, the easier it will be to convert those subscribers into repeat customers.

Every email you send to your list should directly work towards strengthening your brand's recognition for value. This means that you must be extremely careful with the kinds of products you promote as well as the quality of the products you endorse.

Whether you are the developer or not, if you give it your stamp of approval, your subscriber base will hold you accountable should the product or service fail to deliver. You should therefore always review each product or offer you are planning to promote so that you can not only stand behind it but can directly answer any questions that your subscribers may have about the offer.

Keep your emails focused and relevant. If you end up venturing into a new niche or are interested in exploring other markets, you should work towards creating individual segmented lists for each niche.

Segment Your Lists For Better Targeting!
Segmenting your lists does more than maximise your chances of having your emails delivered successfully. List segmenting will also help you effectively communicate and target specific subscribers, increasing response rates and helping you create successful broadcasts.

For example, if you developed a mailing list catering to the "Internet Marketing" crowd, your subscribers likely come from different backgrounds, are currently at varying levels of their marketing training or are interested in various areas of the Internet Marketing industry.

By segmenting your lists, you can create content based on each group's interests and skill levels as well as develop products and services around each subscriber category.

Don't Let Your Lists Run Cold!
It would help if you focused on staying in constant communication with your subscriber base. This doesn't mean that you necessarily have to email them every day, but what you want to do is consider creating a posting schedule so that you can get into the habit of connecting with your subscribers regularly while demonstrating consistency.

CONCLUSION

Your subscribers will then begin to expect your emails on certain days, and by doing this, you will start to see a dramatic increase in your open rates. The more consistent you are with your broadcasts, the easier it will be to condition your subscribers to accept promotional based emails and advertisements in between mailings containing free content and resources.